Rudy the
Rhinoceros

by Jan Latta

Reading consultant: Susan Nations, M.Ed., author/literacy coach/consultant in literacy development

Science and curriculum consultant: Debra Voege, M.A., science and math curriculum resource teacher

GARETH**STEVENS**
GS
PUBLISHING
A Member of the WRC Media Family of Companies

Hello! My name is Rudy, and I am a rhinoceros. My **ancestors** lived on Earth about sixty million years ago.

There are five **species**, or types, of rhinos.

Two species live in Africa. The black rhino has a hooked lip. The white rhino's lip is squared. Despite their names, the color of their skin is not different. Both are the same grayish color as all rhinos.

Three species of rhinos are named after three places in Asia — Java, Sumatra, and India.

Sumatran and Javan rhinos are very **rare**.

Indian rhinos have large folds of bumpy skin. They look like they are wearing **armor** plates.

I am a Black rhino. I have a lot in common with my cousins. We all live in hot places and enjoy the shade.

When rhinos are born, we weigh as much as
110 pounds (50 kilograms). Our mothers are very
caring. A rhino mom looks after her baby for two
to five years until she has another baby. After we
leave our mom, we usually live on our own.

We start to grow our horns when we are two to three months old. When we are about six years old, our horns are big enough to use to dig up food from the ground. Our horns are also strong enough to dig up the roots of bushes and knock over trees.

Our horns are made of the same material as your hair and fingernails. No other animal has horns on its nose.

Sometimes, big males fight with their horns. They are trying to see which rhino is stronger. A horn might get knocked off. Luckily, it can grow back.

All rhinos are **herbivores**. We eat the buds, shoots, and leaves of plants. I use my hooked lip like a finger to grab leaves.

White rhinos scoop up food with their square lips.
All rhinos need to drink plenty of water. We can use
our horns to dig for water.

We have a good sense of smell, and we hear very well.

Our eyesight is very bad.

Our poor eyesight sometimes causes us to make mistakes. We might **charge** at trees or rocks, thinking they are enemies! We can run 35 miles (56 kilometers) per hour. It is easy for us to outrun humans.

Rhinos have three toes on each foot. Our middle toe supports most of our weight. White rhinos are the heaviest of the five species. They can weigh up to 6,013 pounds (2,727 kilograms)!

We can make a lot of noise! We growl, grunt, puff, squeal, and bellow.

We also **communicate** by spraying our scent on grass, bushes, and trees. Other animals can smell this.

We love to take a bath in the mud! We cover ourselves in mud to stay cool in the heat.

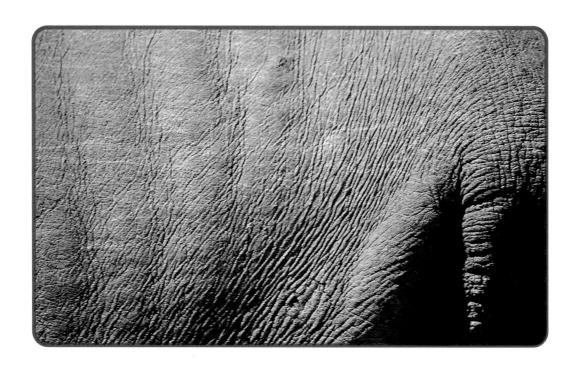

Mud is healthy for our thick skin. It keeps flies and other insects from biting us.

We have little helpers, too. Birds called oxpeckers, or **tick** birds, eat the ticks on our skin. These insects can hurt us! Oxpeckers also screech loudly to warn us of danger, such as a tiger trying to hunt rhino babies.

Rhinos can live up to sixty years. Today, there are fewer than eighteen thousand rhinos left in the world. People destroy our **habitat** and hunt us for our horns.

Humans are the biggest danger to us. Luckily, some people work very hard to help our wild animal family continue.

Rhinoceros Facts

Did You Know?

• The word "rhinoceros" comes from Greek. *Rhino* means "nose," and *ceros* means "horn."

• Rhinos can live in many kinds of places. They can live in hot, dry grasslands called savannas. They can also live in forests or swampy areas.

• Black, White, and Sumatran rhinos have two horns. Indian and Javan rhinos have one horn.

• The longest horn on record belonged to a White rhino. It measured 62 inches (158 centimeters) long.

• In the Middle East, people use rhino horns to make handles for daggers. In Asia, people crush the horns into powder to use in medicines.

• In some countries, people catch rhinos and cut off their horns to protect the rhino's life. Without horns, these rhinos will not be bothered by hunters.

• Rhinos can live thirty to sixty years.

• Rhinos are very good swimmers.

• Rhinos do not sweat.

• Sumatran rhinos are the only species of rhino that has hair.

Map — Where Rhinoceros Live

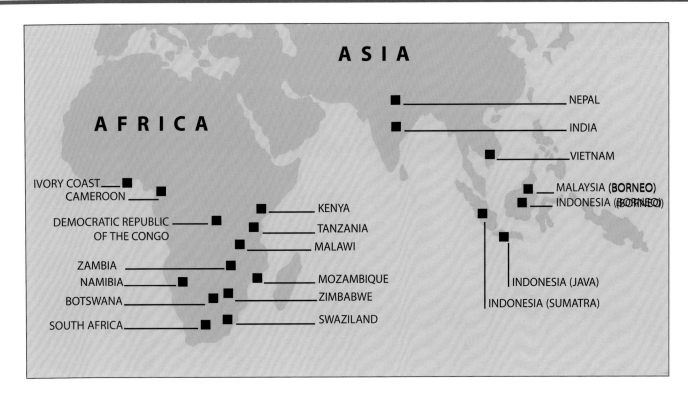

ASIA

AFRICA

NEPAL

INDIA

VIETNAM

IVORY COAST

CAMEROON

MALAYSIA (BORNEO)

INDONESIA (BORNEO)

DEMOCRATIC REPUBLIC OF THE CONGO

KENYA

TANZANIA

MALAWI

ZAMBIA

NAMIBIA

MOZAMBIQUE

BOTSWANA

ZIMBABWE

INDONESIA (JAVA)

INDONESIA (SUMATRA)

SOUTH AFRICA

SWAZILAND

Glossary

ancestors — relatives that lived long before one's parents were born

armor — sheets of metal worn to protect against attack

charge — to run toward something very fast to attack it

communicate — to send messages to others

habitat — the environment, or place, where an animal lives

herbivores — animals that eat only plants

rare — not common or usual; not seen very often

species — types of an animal

tick — a small insect that attaches to an animal and sucks its blood

More Information

Books

Black Rhino. Animals in Danger (series). Rod Theodorou
  (Heinemann Library)

Oh Look, It's a Nosserus. African Stories (series).
  Kate Noble and Rachel Bass (Silver Seahorse)

Woolly Rhinoceros. Prehistoric Animals Set II (series).
  Michael P. Goecke (Buddy Books)

Web Sites

Kids' Planet
www.kidsplanet.org/factsheets/rhinoceros.html
Get fun facts about rhinos.

National Geographic for Kids: Rhinos
www.nationalgeographic.com/kids/creature_feature/0205/rhinos.html
Send a post card, listen to audio, watch videos, and find fun facts about rhinos.

Publisher's note to educators and parents: Our editors have carefully reviewed these Web sites to ensure that they are suitable for children. Many Web sites change frequently, however, and we cannot guarantee that a site's future contents will continue to meet our high standards of quality and educational value. Be advised that children should be closely supervised whenever they access the Internet.

Please visit our Web site at: **www.garethstevens.com**
For a free color catalog describing Gareth Stevens Publishing's
list of high-quality books and multimedia programs,
call 1-800-542-2595 (USA) or 1-800-387-3178 (Canada).
Gareth Stevens Publishing's fax: (414) 332-3567.

Library of Congress Cataloging-in-Publication Data

Latta, Jan.
    Rudy the rhinoceros / by Jan Latta. — North American ed.
      p. cm. — (Wild animal families)
    Includes bibliographical references.
    ISBN-13: 978-0-8368-7771-7 (lib. bdg.)
    ISBN-13: 978-0-8368-7778-6 (softcover)
    1. Rhinoceroses—Juvenile literature. I. Title.
QL737.U63L37 2007
599.66'8—dc22   2006032128

This North American edition first published in 2007 by
Gareth Stevens Publishing
A Member of the WRC Media Family of Companies
330 West Olive Street, Suite 100
Milwaukee, WI 53212 USA

This U.S. edition copyright © 2007 by Gareth Stevens, Inc.
Original edition and photographs copyright © 2005 by Jan Latta.
First produced as *Adventures with Rufus the Rhinoceros* by
TRUE TO LIFE BOOKS, 12b Gibson Street, Bronte, NSW 2024 Australia

Acknowledgements: The author thanks Kathy and Karl Ammann in Africa, who helped make this book possible. And Jon Resnick who generously allowed reproduction of his photographs on pages 3, 8, and 19.

Project editor: Jan Latta
Design: Jan Latta

Gareth Stevens editorial direction: Valerie J. Weber
Gareth Stevens editor: Tea Benduhn
Gareth Stevens art direction: Tammy West
Gareth Stevens Graphic designer: Scott Krall
Gareth Stevens production: Jessica Yanke and Robert Kraus

Printed in Canada

1 2 3 4 5 6 7 8 9 10 10 09 08 07 06